# THE APARTMENT MAINTENANCE HANDBOOK

**By: Eric Flynn**

# MAINTENANCE HANDBOOK

## TABLE OF CONTENTS


### FAIR HOUSING

Fair Housing
The Fair Housing Act
Additional Protection if You Have a Disability
Housing Opportunities for Families
Guidelines for Non-Discriminatory Leasing
Definition of Family
Definition of Handicapped
Vocabulary
Laws Pertaining to the Handicapped
Steering
Occupancy Policy
Fair Housing and Service Requests

### ORGANIZING THE MAINTENANCE DEPARTMENT

Organizing the Maintenance Department
Maintenance Shop Standards
Organizing the Maintenance Shop
Organizational Tools
Property Site Information

### MAKE READY MAINTENANCE

Make Ready Maintenance
Make Ready Maintenance
Make Ready Checklists
Make Ready Board
Maintenance Make Ready Instructions
Standards for Apartment Painting
Apartment Painting Specifications
Standards for Apartment Cleaning
Apartment Cleaning Specifications
Carpet Replacement/Shampoo
Final Inspection

**KEY AND LOCK GUIDELINES**

Key and Lock Guidelines
Issuing Keys to New Residents
Returning Keys Upon Move-Out
Key Documentation
Release of Keys to Vendors
Make Ready Lock System (Red Locks)
Lockouts
Lock Changes

**MAINTENANCE REPORTING**

Maintenance Reporting
Maintenance Reports
Weekly Exterior Checklist
Preventative Maintenance
Preventative Maintenance Checklist

**ENERGY CONSERVATION**

Energy Conservation
Vacant Utility Usage
House Lighting
Domestic Hot Water
Major Mechanical
Clubhouse Utilities
Exterior Plumbing

**RESIDENT SERVICES**

Resident Services
The Importance of Service to Our Residents
The Service Request Process
Maintenance Emergencies

**SWIMMING POOL MAINTENANCE**

Swimming Pool Maintenance
Swimming Pool Maintenance Scheduling
Daily Care
Basic Pool Maintenance
Filter Systems
The Mechanics of Pool Filtration
Algae Control
Water Chemistry and Chemicals
General Rules Regarding The Use of Chemicals

**HAZARD COMMUNICATION PROGRAM**

Purpose of Hazard Communication Program

Container Labeling
Material Safety Data Sheets
Employee Information and Training
List of Hazardous Chemicals
Hazards of Non-Routine Tasks
On-Site Contractors
Access to Written Program
Hazard Determination Procedures


**HAZARD COMMUNICATION GLOSSARY**

## FAIR HOUSING

After studying this section, you will:

- Know how to perform your daily duties without discriminating.

- Learn more about laws pertaining to the handicapped.

- Learn how to use the correct vocabulary.

- Understand the definition of "family" and "handicapped."

## THE FAIR HOUSING ACT

The Fair Housing Act prohibits discrimination in housing because of:

- Race

- Color

- National Origin

- Religion

- Sex

- Familial status (including children under the age of 18 living with parents or legal custodians, pregnant women and people securing custody of children under 18)

- Handicap

WHAT HOUSING IS COVERED?

The Fair Housing Act covers most housing.  In some circumstances, the Act exempts owner occupied buildings with no more than four units, single-family housing sold or rented without the use of a broker and housing operated by organizations and private clubs that limit occupancy to members.

WHAT IS PROHIBITED?

**In the Sale and Rental of Housing:**  No one may take any of the following actions based on race, color, national origin, religion, sex, familial status or handicap:

- Refuse to rent or sell housing

- Refuse to negotiate for housing

- Make housing unavailable

- Deny a dwelling

- Set different terms, conditions or privileges for sale or rental of a dwelling

- Provide different housing services or facilities

- Falsely deny that housing is available for inspection, sale or rental

- For profit, persuade owners to sell or rent (blockbusting) or

- Deny anyone access to or membership in a facility or service (such as a multiple listing service) related to the sale or rental of housing

## ADDITIONAL PROTECTION IF YOU HAVE A DISABLITIY

If a resident or prospect:

- Has a physical or mental disability (including hearing, mobility and visual impairments, chronic alcoholism, chronic mental illness, AIDS, AIDS Related Complex and mental retardation) that substantially limits one or more major life activities,

- Has a record of such a disability, or

- Is regarded as having such a disability.

A landlord may not:

- Refuse to let the resident make reasonable modifications to the dwelling or common-use areas, **at the resident's expense**, if necessary for the handicapped person to use the housing. (Where reasonable, the landlord may permit changes only if the resident agrees to restore the property to its original condition when he/she moves.)

- Refuse to make reasonable accommodations in rules, policies, practices or services if necessary for the handicapped person to use the housing.

    **Example:** A building with a "no pets" policy must allow a visually impaired resident to keep a guide dog.

    **Example:** An apartment community that offers residents ample, unassigned parking must honor a request from a mobility-impaired resident for a reserved space near his or her apartment if necessary to assure that he/she can have access to the apartment.

However, housing need not be made available to a person who is a direct threat to the health or safety of others or who currently uses illegal drugs.

## HOUSING OPPORTUNITIES FOR FAMILIES

Unless a building or community qualifies as housing only for older persons, its leasing requirements may not discriminate based on a familial status. That is, the requirements may not discriminate against families in which one or more children under 18 live with:

- A parent

- A person who has legal custody of the child or the children

- The designee of the parent or legal custodian, with the parent or custodian's written permission.

Familial status protection also applies to pregnant women and anyone securing legal custody of a child under the age of 18.

The Apartment Maintenance Handbook by Eric Flynn

**Exemption:** Housing for older persons is exempt from the prohibition against familial status discrimination if:

- The HUD secretary has determined that it is specifically designed for and occupied by elderly persons under a federal, state or local government program, or

- It is occupied solely by persons who are 62 or older, or

- It houses at least one person who is 55 or older in at least 80% of the occupied units; has significant services and facilities for older persons; and adheres to a published policy statement that demonstrates intent to house persons who are 55 and older. The requirement for significant services and facilities is waived if providing them is not practicable and the housing is necessary to provide important housing opportunities for older persons.

A transition period permits residents on or before September 13, 1988, to continue living in the housing, regardless of their age, without interfering with the exemption.

Quoted from Fair Housing, It's Your Right published by U.S. Department of Housing and Urban Development, Office of Fair Housing and Equal Opportunity (HUD-1260-FHEO, July 1990).

# GUIDELINES FOR NON-DISCRIMINATORY LEASING

## STATEMENT OF RENTAL POLICY

It is company policy (and a law of the United States of America) that any discrimination based on the following criteria is prohibited. Review the Non-Discriminatory Operating Policies Acknowledgement in the Sample Forms section.

Under no circumstances shall the following be reasons for refusing housing:

- Race
- Color
- National Origin
- Religion
- Sex
- Physical or Mental Disability
- Familial Status

If you, as an employee, feel you have been harassed or discriminated against, contact your Property Supervisor.

Discrimination is also prohibited when dealing with current residents. Review the Fair Housing Compliance Checklist in the Sample Forms section.

## DEFINITION OF FAMILY

A family is defined in the Fair Housing Amendments Act of 1988 as one or more individuals under the age of 18 years being domiciled with:

- A parent or another person having legal custody of such individual(s), or

- A designee of such parent with the written permission of such parent.

A person who is pregnant or in the process of obtaining legal custody of a person under 18 years of age must be treated as a family.

## DEFINITION OF HANDICAPPED

A person who has a physical or mental impairment which substantially limits one or more of that person's major life functions, which include caring for oneself, performing manual tasks, walking, seeing, hearing, speaking, breathing, learning or working.

## VOCABULARY

Effective March 12, 1989, the words "all-adult", "adult area", "family area", "family pool", "family section", "adults only", "family (or adult) oriented", "adult (or family) living", must be deleted from your leasing vocabulary.

Pools have rules for the enjoyment of all residents. There are no "family sections", as families and adults must be offered the same rental units without distinction.

Notice also that the statement of rental specifies "occupants." If two persons are permitted in a one bedroom apartment, the following are **examples** of two occupants:

- Married couple
- Two roommates (same or opposite sex)
- Mother and child under 18
- Father and child under 18
- Legal guardian and child under 18

## LAWS PERTAINING TO THE HANDICAPPED

If a handicapped person wants to move into a property, that person has the right to do so. If modifications to the entry or the interior of the apartment are necessary, <u>the handicapped person must pay for such changes</u>. Examples of such modifications would include ramps, grab bars in bathrooms, wider door openings, and lower light switches. Management has the right to approve such changes to be certain that they will conform to building codes. A handicapped person may also make changes to common areas (pools, laundry rooms, and mail rooms, for example) under the same rules that he or she <u>pay for such changes with management's prior written approval.</u>

**The handicapped person will also be required to restore the premises to a reasonable condition upon moving out of the property.**
**Does the law mean that I will have to lease to all families and all handicapped persons?**

**No.** Standards for living at the property must be applied equally. A prospect's credit rating, prior history and employment standards still apply. It is not discrimination if someone (or family or handicapped person) has a bad prior residence history and you reject them. You will be discriminating if you don't apply these laws equally to all prospects.

## STEERING

Steering is an attempt to refer prospects to:

- other properties,
- certain buildings or areas within your property, or
- areas on the property such as playgrounds, busy roads, etc.

The following are examples of Steering (Wrong) and the same statements rephrased in a nondiscriminatory way (Right):

### WRONG

Walking from the information center to the model, you say, "Most of our families live near the playground."

### RIGHT

"We have a playground located near the mail room.  Let me show it to you."

### WRONG

"The schools serving our properties are lousy."

### RIGHT

Offer factual information about locations of schools or school bus stops, but do not offer subjective information about a school's quality or reputation. Encourage the prospect to visit the schools from sources other than you.

### WRONG

"Most families don't want to live… (near a busy street, next to the creek, on the third floor)."

### RIGHT

"…is a heavily traveled street."

**Can children of the opposite sex share a bedroom?**

The Apartment Maintenance Handbook by Eric Flynn

**Yes.** This is a parent's decision, not yours or the company's.  We can only establish occupancy limitation (i.e., number of persons in an apartment).

## Can we still have "specials"?

**Yes.**  All specials must be in writing, documented and offered to everyone. A verbal special is potentially very dangerous because there is no way to prove that such a special was offered to every prospect. Rather than use phrases such as "Ask me about our specials", we need to be specific (e.g.; $20 off all 3rd floor one-bedrooms, expires April 30th).

For this reason, it is important to update the rental schedule on a regular basis.

## How do rules regarding bicycles apply?

The resident policies state that riding bicycles or motorcycles on sidewalks is prohibited. This applies to all residents – children and adults.

## Can we limit families to the first floor?

**No.**  This is discriminatory. Which floor to live on is a prospect's decision.

## Can a handicapped person have a parking space in front of his/her apartment?

**Yes,** if that person will pay for the signs and markings.

## Why was the law changed to add families and the handicapped as protected classes?

The Fair Housing Amendments Act had three goals:

- Give HUD authority and power to enforce existing fair-housing laws.

- Make more housing available to families (and the homeless) as it is perceived that there is a shortage of such housing.

- Broaden protection of housing rights for the handicapped.

## What are the penalties for discrimination?

A person who can prove discrimination can receive damages awarded by a federal court or an administrative law judge. A company will be fined $10,000 for the first offense, $25,000 for the second offense and $50,000 for the third offense.

---

**A Leasing Consultant or other on-site employees can also be found personally liable for equal fines.**

---

**Are older persons forced to live with families and young children?**

The Fair Housing Amendment Act of 1988 creates two exceptions based on:

- A community where all persons are over the age of 62, or

- At least 1 person in each unit is over 55 and certain services exist and activities offered to cater to these people.

**Can we offer senior citizen discounts?**

**Yes**, if senior citizen discounts are part of your leasing policy and are applied equally to all seniors.

**Does this apply to verification procedures?**

**Yes**, in two important ways:

- First, you must make a note of the person's name you spoke with to obtain prior residence or employment information. Make detailed notes, especially if an applicant's history is poor.

- Second, all prospect leasing information must be retained for 2 ½ years. This is because the person who thinks he or she may have been discriminated against has up to 2 years to file a complaint with HUD. Holding the file for 30 months puts us safely past any processing delays within HUD after a complaint has been filed.

---

**REMEMBER: Do not discriminate; do not steer prospects; do treat all persons equally; and know our statement of rental policy and other policies.**

---

## OCCUPANCY POLICY

According to the Fair Housing Amendment Act of 1988, Section 100.10 (A) (3), Owner is permitted to allow reasonable limitations on occupancy, as long as these limitations are applied to all occupants and do not discriminate on the basis of race, color, national origin, religion, sex, handicap or familial status.

Check with local city ordinance for additional protected classes.

## FAIR HOUSING AND SERVICE REQUESTS

Under no circumstances should you refuse to work in a resident's apartment for the following reasons:

- Race
- Color
- National Origin
- Religion
- Sex
- Physical or Mental Disability
- Disabled Veterans
- Familial Status

All service requests should be completed in the order in which they are received. The exceptions are emergency work orders, work orders requiring parts to be ordered or work orders requiring an outside vendor. In these cases, the following procedures are to be followed:

- Make a note on the work order of the exact reason for the delay, including the date and time.

- Contact the resident or have an office employee contact the resident to explain the reason for the delay.

- Never make promises to a resident if you are unsure of when the work order will be complete.

On the rare instance where you are beginning to become back-logged with pending work orders, the following procedures are to be followed:

- Contact the Property Manager and explain the reason for the delay, if he or she is not already aware.

- Office employees should contact the residents with pending work orders and explain the delay.

- Notes should be made on each work order of the call, the employee's name, date and time.

Notes/Comments:

## ORGANIZING THE MAINTENANCE DEPARTMENT

After studying this section, you will:

- Understand typical maintenance shop standards
- Be able to organize the maintenance shop
- Become more organized and efficient

## MAINTENANCE SHOP STANDARDS

All onsite maintenance shops should be organized in accordance with the following:

- A minimum of 1-week inventory should be maintained.

- All shelves can be labeled and painted these color codes:

| | |
|---|---|
| Plumbing | Red |
| Appliances | Green |
| Electrical | Yellow |
| Punch-Out | Orange |
| Tools Storage | Brown |
| HVAC | Blue |
| Walls/Ceilings | White |
| Floors | Grey |

- All parts Should be separated and kept in bin boxes. These boxes should be labeled with the individual part name, part number and quantity of this part to be kept on hand. Most supply companies will provide these bins and educate you on set up and implementation.

- <u>All shops must ALWAYS be locked when not occupied by an employee!</u> The shop should NEVER be left open when maintenance personnel are out.

- All shops Should have:

  - ☐ Maps / property layouts
  - ☐ Preventative maintenance schedule.
  - ☐ A copy of the safety checklist from this manual.
  - ☐ Material Safety Data Sheets (MSDS) organizer for chemicals and materials used on the property.
  - ☐ A fully charged fire extinguisher must be kept in plain view.
  - ☐ A smoke detector.
  - ☐ A first aid kit.
  - ☐ An eye wash station.
  - ☐ A list of emergency telephone numbers.
  - ☐ A vented door.

## ORGANIZING THE MAINTENANCE SHOP

Your maintenance shop must be organized. Most supply companies have an organized bin system and will assist you in its implementation and proper use.

- A regular accounting of your stock must be made so you will know what to order and when to place an order.

- You should have a 1-week inventory of the most commonly used parts and supplies on your property.

- If you are assigned to a property with substandard stock, make a list of the items you need to build your inventory and present it to your Property Manager for approval.

- Reorder on a regular basis to keep your stock up. <u>You do not want residents waiting for service because we do not have the parts to make repairs.</u>

- Be budget conscious and plan ahead. Communicate with your Manager on a regular basis and before ordering stock to ensure you stay within budget.

## ORGANIZATIONAL TOOLS

The apartment business is a busy one. The work load can sometimes feel overwhelming, especially if you are not organized. Our there can be several tools to help keep you organized. They include:

- Inventory Control Log
- Property Site Information
- Make Ready Board
- Supply Request Form
- Various Checklists
- Preventative Maintenance Checklists

It is up to you to provide the initiative to use these tools and systems to gain maximum productivity.

These tools will be discussed further in subsequent sections of the Maintenance Handbook.

## PROPERTY SITE INFORMATION

It is good practice that every property have two copies of the following maps. One copy is to be kept in an accessible place located in the maintenance shop. The other copy will be kept in the office.

These maps should be separate maps and no attempt should be made to combine them. They are to be clearly legible, laminated and kept up to date at all times.

1. Natural gas shutoffs
2. Water shutoffs
3. Master water meter locations
4. Main water lines
5. Sprinkler system main cutoffs
6. Fire hydrant locations
7. Sewer cleanouts and main runs
8. Electrical shutoffs and transformers
9. Exterior lighting control locations
10. Swimming pool operation and valves (schematic)
11. Fire alarm pull station locations and main control panels
12. Television cable line runs
13. Plot map showing property lines and easements
14. Emergency controls for access gates (if applicable)
15. Master telephone boxes

Any employee who is handling after hours and weekend maintenance calls should be completely familiar with and have access to the property site information.

## MAKE READY MAINTENANCE

After studying this section, you will:

- Understand the importance of make-readies to the success of your property

- Know what is expected of the maintenance department regarding make-readies

- Learn the importance of communication during the make-ready process

> "If we don't have ready product we may as well turn off the lights and go home.
> At least we'd save on payroll."
>
> -Eric Flynn, President
> Apartment Medic LLC

## MAKE READY MAINTENANCE

One of the main functions of the maintenance department on an apartment community is to make vacant apartments ready for occupancy. Our goal is to have all units ready on every community. Your ready apartments should be clean, attractive and well maintained.

The primary tool for scheduling and communicating about make ready units is typically the Make Ready Board. Always utilize the make ready checklists to record work done in each make ready apartment. Upon full completion of the make ready, the apartment must be walked by the manager.

Remember: if you do not satisfy the resident with the condition of the apartment upon move in, it will be difficult to satisfy them throughout their stay at your community.

## MAKE READY CHECKLISTS

There are 3 checklists to be completed by appropriate personnel for each make ready.

- The Maintenance Checklist
- The Painter's Checklist
- The Housekeeper's Checklist

Review the Maintenance Checklist, Painter's Checklist and Housekeeper's Checklist in the Sample Forms section.

Whether the work is done in house or through a contractor, these checklists must be filled out by the person completing the work and turned in to the Manager. These systematic checklists allow for greater organization and virtually eliminates time wasted retrieving supplies.

By following these steps you will save time and energy traveling back and forth between the shop and spend more time in the apartment completing the work.

- Walk through the apartment on your first inspection.
- Make notes on work that needs to be done, listing all parts needed.
- Make one trip to the maintenance shop to retrieve the parts and supplies needed to complete the make ready.

The Apartment Maintenance Handbook by Eric Flynn

## MAKE-READY BOARD

The MAKE READY BOARD is usually located in the Management Office. This board is an organized chart of every apartment that needs to be made ready, either for a pending move-in date or a future lease. Across the top of the board the following categories are printed: (Review the Make Ready Board Form in the Sample Forms section)

- Unit Number
- Move-Out Date
- Date of Inspection
- Move-In Date
- Trash Removal
- Sheet Rock
- Paint
- Maintenance
- Vinyl
- Blinds
- Carpet
- Appliances
- Clean
- Locks Changed
- Final Manager Inspection
- Comments

An apartment should be listed on the board when the Notice to Vacate has been received so that the entire team is aware of upcoming turn-over activity. It is a good policy that vacancies must be made ready for occupancy within 3 to 5 days at maximum.

You must review the Make-Ready Board regularly with the office team and update it throughout the day. Communicate immediately problems that arise in the make-ready, especially those that will result in a delay getting the apartment ready for move in.

- Complete your notes on the Make-Ready Checklist. Review the Make Ready Checklist in the Sample Forms section.

- If you notice work in the apartment that will take longer than usual, i.e. water damage, vinyl repair, construction issues, etc., radio or go to the office and communicate this information to the manager before beginning the work.

- Make appropriate notes on the Make-Ready Board regarding scheduled dates of work, completion dates and any other important information. (Examples include carpet replacement, appliance replacement, major repairs, dates of scheduled work, etc.)

- As the work is completed check it off the Make-Ready Board when the checklist is turned in.

Communicate to the office any scheduling changes or delays. This will allow the office team to communicate with the future resident for move in dates and times, eliminating conflict.

## MAINTENANCE MAKE-READY INSTRUCTIONS

Outlines designed to help the Maintenance Team develop an efficient and thorough approach to maintenance make-ready are included here. These provide a detailed guide of what to check and how to check it. Subsequently, the outlines tells how to fix many of the more common problems that you may encounter.

### KEYS

- All units should have a keyless knob and a regular deadbolt.

- Make sure there are enough keys for each resident plus 2 extras.

- Make sure all keys operate the lock without unnecessary jiggling.

### DOORS

- Inspect the door's facing to make sure it isn't damaged and also check if the door needs weather stripping or painting.

## PRELIMINARY WATER CHECK

### TOILETS

- As soon as you're inside the apartment, turn off the water supply to the toilets.

- With a wax pencil, make a mark inside the tank showing where the water level is. You should also check whether it looks like the water level is going above the overflow.

## APPLIANCES

### REFRIGERATOR

- To check if the refrigerator is cooling, place a thermometer in the freezer section. The temperature range should be from 6°F to 18°F, depending on the type of refrigerator and the year it was produced.

- Examine the door gasket. To check for a positive seal, insert a dollar bill between the door gasket and the box and close the door. The seal is OK if you feel a slight resistance when you pull the bill out.

### RANGE

- Turn on the oven, broiler and each of the top burners separately to "high." If the range is electric, the element should glow bright red.

- Operate the vent hood. Make sure that the light operates, that the fan draws air and that the filter is clean.

The Apartment Maintenance Handbook by Eric Flynn

### DISPOSAL

- Turn on the disposal and listen carefully for objects that may cause it to lock up later.

- If the noise level is high, use a flashlight to check and see that the blades aren't broken.

### DISHWASHER

- Operate the dishwasher through a complete cycle and check that no water is leaking from:

- Around the motor
- The hot water supply line
- The drain line
- Around the door gasket

- Check that the drying element operates properly.

- If the door latch does not operate easily, WD-40 helps on hard-to-operate latches.

- Make sure the racks are in good condition and fit snugly.

## KITCHEN – GENERAL

### FAUCETS

- Inspect the kitchen faucet for leaks in the packing or O-ring near the stem or spout.

- Make sure that water is not going under the seal between the faucet and the sink.

- If the faucet drips at all, replace the washers.

### DRAINS

- Run water while inspecting the drain piping under the sink.

- To check the drain lines for weak areas that might leak later, tap them with the handle of a screwdriver.

### COUNTERTOPS

- If the counter top has a large damaged area that was caused by a hot pot or general abuse, report it to your Manager and discuss alternatives i.e. removing the damaged area and replacing it with a cutting board, or resurfacing.

- If the caulking on the counter top is cracked or looks bad, remove the old caulk and redo it.

## CABINETS

• Check that the kitchen cabinets and drawers open and shut easily and that the cabinets stay shut.

# BATHROOM

## SINK & VANITY

- Check the faucet and if you detect any drips, replace all washers.

- Examine the sink for chips in the porcelain. If the sink is chipped, report it to your Manager and discuss alternatives.

- Run water as you check for leaks under the sink. Also, tap the drain lines with the handle of a screwdriver and check for weak areas that might start leaking later.

- If the caulking on the vanity top is cracked or looks bad, remove the old caulk and redo it.

- If the top of the vanity is made of corian or synthetic marble, use the following procedures for removing stains:

- For light stains or surface burns, use toothpaste and fine steel wool to scrub the stain out.

- For heavy stains, use 600 grit wet and dry sandpaper and sand the area until the stain is removed. It's a good idea to use a sanding block with the sandpaper, since this will prevent you from leaving a deep impression in the top. While sanding, keep the area wet so the sandpaper doesn't get clogged.

- Once either type of stain has been removed, apply car rubbing compound to the area with a small buffer that's attached to a hand drill. This will smooth out any scratches made by the steel wool or sanding cloth.

- If the top of the vanity is made of Formica, you can attempt to remove stains or burns using the following procedures:

- For light stains or surface burns, use very fine steel wool to scrub the stain or burn out.

## TOILETS

- When you first entered the apartment, you shut the water supply off and marked the water level in the tank. At that point, if it looked like the water was going into the overflow – it was! In this situation, you must either adjust or replace the ballcock.

- After the water supply to the tank has been shut off for at least an hour, check the water level again. If the water level has dropped at all from the mark you made, you either have a leak, the flapper is out of adjustment or the flush valve seal is worn.

- Flappers can either be out of alignment or they can deteriorate to the point where they leak. To detect a deteriorated flapper, rub your fingers along the seating area. If you feel any pitted areas, that's a sure sign of a deteriorated flapper. Also, deteriorated flappers will turn your finger pitch black. If the flapper has deteriorated, it must be replaced. However, if the flapper is not deteriorated but seems to be leaking, it probably just needs to be adjusted. When you replace a flapper, purchase a good-quality flapper, since cheap flappers wear out too quickly.

## TUBS AND/OR SHOWERS

- Inspect the caulking around the tub or shower. If it is cracked or looks bad, remove the old caulk and redo it. If there is ceramic tile around the tub or shower, check the condition of the caulking very carefully. If the caulking is bad and water gets behind the tile, it will rot the wood or weaken the plaster, which will cause the tiles to fall off the wall.

- Check that the tub holds water and that the water drains out properly. If the water seems to be draining out too slowly, check for a clog in the drain.

- Inspect the tub or shower for chips in the porcelain and report any that you find to the Manager and discuss alternatives.

- If the shower or tub has doors, make sure that they work smoothly. If there is not a shower or tub enclosure, make sure there is a shower curtain rod that is properly secured.

- Check the faucet for leaks and repair any that you find.

- Examine the shower stem for leaks and replace the packing if you find any. When you repair the stem, use waterproof grease. This grease will make it easier to turn the water off and repair the stem the next time it needs it.

- Operate the shower and check for an uneven spray pattern. Cleaning the shower head should solve this problem.

## HEATING AND AIR CONDITIONING

### BOTH

- Change the filter and inspect the coil for any blockage. Clean the coil with a coil cleaner as prescribed by the manufacturer.

- Be sure the thermostat is level and that it is properly secured to the wall. Bad alignment of the thermostat causes improper cycling of the heating or cooling unit.

### HEATING

- During the heating season, turn the thermostat to the heating mode and check the operation of the unit. Take a thermometer reading of the supply air and record it on the Make-Ready Checklist. (NOTE: Always keep in mind most units have a time-delayed fan.)

### AIR CONDITIONING

- During the air conditioning season, turn the thermostat to the cooling position and check the operation of the unit. Take thermometer readings of the supply and return air and record them on the checklist. (16° to 20° coil split)

- CAUTION: When you're checking the air conditioning, do NOT switch the thermostat from cool to off and then back to cool without waiting at least 5 minutes! The compressor needs this much time to equalize its pressure before you can start it again.

- ALWAYS turn the thermostat off after you've checked the air conditioning. (NOTE: The reason for this is that air conditioning units are the largest consumers of electricity in the apartment industry.)

- Use the MAKE READY AIR CONDITIONING CHECKLIST form in conjunction with the Make-Ready Checklist. Every unit must have air conditioning preventative maintenance completed and the form filled in appropriately. Maintain a copy of this form in the Preventative Maintenance Files. (Review the Make Ready Air Conditioning Checklist Form in the Sample Forms section)

### WINDOWS & PATIO DOORS

- Check for broken or badly cracked glass. If you find a pane that needs to be replaced, note its location and dimensions on the Make-Ready Checklist.

- Make sure all windows that are supposed to have screens have them and that the screens are in good condition and are properly secured to their frames.

- Inspect around each window to see if you can feel air entering the apartment through the window frames or around the glass. If you do, either weather-strip or re-caulk around the windows.

- Open and close the windows and patio door to make sure they operate properly. Check that when they are closed you can engage the window and patio door locks with minimum effort.

The Apartment Maintenance Handbook by Eric Flynn

- Check all locks, Charlie bars and pin locks.

## WATER HEATER – ELECTRIC OR GAS

- Make sure that the water heater is set at between 130° and 140°F. If it isn't, adjust it either up or down.

- Check that the pop-off or temperature-pressure valve (T&P valve) is working correctly since this will waste an immeasurable amount of water if it isn't. To check it, grasp the pipe about 6" past the outlet of the valve. If, when you touch the pipe, it feels hot to the touch or if you can feel water flowing through the pipe, the T&P valve is not setting properly. When the T&P valve is relatively new you can usually correct this problem by pulling up on the test lever, which is located on the top of the valve, and allow a free flow of water through the valve. This should dislodge any foreign material that is caught in the seating area of the T&P valve, which should solve the problem. If this method does not work, you must replace the T&P valve.

## MISCELLANEOUS

### MINI-BLINDS

- Examine all blinds making sure that there are no broken cords or slats. Check that the brackets are securely fastened to the wall and that the blinds open and close easily. Raise and lower the blinds to make sure they work properly. Replace missing or broken slats or note what size blind or slat is needed on the Make Ready Checklist.

### LIGHTS AND SWITCHES

- Check that all bulbs supplied by the community are in working order.

- Make sure that all light switches and wall receptacles work correctly and that all cover plates are in place.

## FINAL WALK-THROUGH

- Once you've completed this visit to the apartment, take a final walk around the apartment. Check to make sure that all the lights are off, that the blinds are closed and that the heat is either off or set at a low temperature (depending on the season and the local weather conditions).

- As you make this final walk-through, you should also go over the Make-Ready Checklist to make sure that you haven't missed anything. Also check that you noted all the extra information you'll need for any other work you'll have to do in the apartment.

- Turn off all breakers – except the refrigerator/freezer. Set the refrigerator/freezer on the warmest setting. (In freezing weather, leave the heater on set at 50°.)

**Remember – it's much easier to work in a vacant apartment than it is in an occupied one. Save yourself the hassles later on and fix it all right now!**

## STANDARDS FOR APARTMENT PAINTING

An apartment must be vacant in order to completely judge the paint.

Experience has indicated that any apartment with over a 6-month occupancy will usually have to have all walls painted; touching up latex paint is usually very obvious. Ceilings do not need painting as often as walls – every 3 to 5 years if they are kept clean near air vents.

## STANDARDS FOR APARTMENT CLEANING

### STANDARDS FOR TILE CARE

- Spray tile to be cleaned with a solution of bleach and water. After allowing tile to soak for a while, brush tile with a hand brush, cleaning out grooves and removing any soap film on the tile.

### STANDARDS FOR FORMICA CARE

- Clean area with a mild abrasive; do not use steel wool.

- After entire area is lightly scrubbed, apply cleaning solution, clean and polish completely.

### STANDARDS FOR CABINET CARE

- Clean with a damp cloth and weak solution of liquid cleaner.

- Lightly polish all exterior cabinet surfaces with lemon oil.

### STANDARDS FOR SERVICING STOVE EXHAUST FAN

- Remove filter and wash thoroughly in a solution of detergent and water; rinse and dry cycle through dishwasher.

## CARPET REPLACEMENT/SHAMPOO

Make sure the carpet vendor is approved through your AVP. The shampoo vendor should follow our standards.

### STANDARDS FOR SPOT CLEANING & STEAM CLEANING CARPETS

- Spot clean as needed with spot cleaning kit.

- Steam clean carpet.

- Rake carpet to raise "nap."

- Average carpet cleaning cost should be $20 unless approved by your AVP.

- All additional costs for repairs, stretches or extra cleaning must be approved by the manager prior to the work being completed.

## FINAL INSPECTION

Final inspection should be made by the Manager at least 48 hours prior to the scheduled move-in.

During the make-ready process, the Office and Maintenance Teams can use the Make-Ready Board to help track the progress of each unit.

The described make-ready process should be followed whenever possible; however, there will be instances when scheduling will need to vary based on your needs.

## KEY AND LOCK GUIDELINES

All employees must strictly adhere to established key guidelines. After studying this section you will:

- Know the process of issuing keys to new residents
- Know the process of returning keys upon move-out
- Learn how to document key releases
- Understand standard policy on releasing keys to vendors
- Know how to implement the ready lock system (red locks)
- Know how to handle lock outs
- Understand standard policy on lock changes

## ISSUING KEYS TO NEW RESIDENTS

When new residents move in, one apartment key per adult resident and one mailbox key per apartment should be issued. Personnel should maintain two keys to each apartment – one for staff or resident use and one spare stored separately and securely. Keys must be stored in locked locations and each key must be tagged and coded. **Never make a key or key tag using the apartment number. Always keep the key codes in a secure location and not open for anyone to see. All key boxes must be kept locked and be behind a locked door.**

## RETURNING KEYS UPON MOVE-OUT

At move-out, all keys should be returned to Management, and personnel should make a notation of the returned keys on the completed Move Out Inventory. If no keys are returned, $25-50 <u>per lock</u> should be charged for rekeying expense.

## KEY DOCUMENTATION

Any time a key is released to a resident, vendor or employee, release must be documented on the Key Check Out Log. This log should be kept in a loose leaf binder adjacent to the key cabinet. Completed log sheets must be filed after each month. Review the Key Check Out Log Form in the Sample Forms section.

If a resident requests a key to be released, the resident must complete an Authorization to Enter form. The completed form should be placed in the resident's active lease file so that all management personnel will have access to it. All authorization forms should be placed in the resident's folder after the key is returned.

- Vendors or Residents should NEVER have access to the key box.

- After move out, the apartment locks should be changed to a red vendor lock. (See instructions below)

- Locks **must** be changed and copies of keys made, coded and hung after all work is completed including the manager's walk through.

If an emergency arises, i.e. flood, fire, etc., a work order must be generated before keys are removed.

## RELEASE OF KEYS TO VENDORS

Before disbursing a key to a vendor/contractor, it is imperative that the Community Key Check-Out Log is completed in its entirety. <u>This policy should be followed without deviation each time a key is disbursed.</u>

## MAKE READY LOCK SYSTEM (RED LOCKS)

- Key all vacancies alike and paint the lock red.

- Upon move-out, immediately replace the lock with a "vacancy lock."

- The vacancy lock must remain on the apartment until the new resident's move in day. This will facilitate last-minute inspections and showings of the unit. **Note: all employees can be taught to change a lock! If maintenance personnel are not available, office staff should be able to change a lock.**

- The only apartment key that a leasing agent, make-ready technician, contractor, etc., will need is a vacancy key.

## LOCKOUTS

The on-call maintenance team should assist residents with lock outs when and if the courtesy officer is not available if your property has one. Residents who are locked out must show proper identification. **Identification should be shown and verified with the lease before the resident enters the apartment.**

## LOCK CHANGES

**NOTE: All requests for lock changes should be in writing.  The request should be filed in the resident file.**

## MAINTENANCE REPORTING

After studying this section you will:

- Understand the importance of Maintenance reporting

- Learn how to use each of these reports

## MAINTENANCE REPORTS

### Weekly Exterior Checklist

- Performed weekly

- Ensures hazards are identified and action is taken to correct them

### Preventative Maintenance Schedule

- You should use monthly schedule issued at the beginning of each month.

- Complete a few items daily so all items are complete before the end of the month.

### Swimming Pool Log

- See the SWIMMING POOL MAINTENANCE section for complete information.

## WEEKLY EXTERIOR CHECKLIST

After the item has been inspected the condition should be logged and initialed by the person inspecting the item.

Use the following abbreviations when logging the condition:

- A – Acceptable

- I – Immediate Attention

- R – Repair Made

- N/A – Not Applicable

Review the Weekly Exterior Checklist Form in the Sample Forms section.

## PREVENTATIVE MAINTENANCE

Preventative maintenance programs saves time and money. The ideal maintenance operation would concentrate on preventative maintenance in order to cut down on the very expensive and time consuming practice of corrective maintenance.

For example, we know it takes less time to add a few drops of oil than to replace a motor. It is also easier to replace a filter than to replace a compressor. Obviously the oil and filter cost much less than the motor or the compressor.

The Preventative Maintenance Checklist is the tool you will use to set your schedule for preventative maintenance. The checklist sets realistic goals for preventative maintenance. This report is due monthly. Consult with your manager for due dates and plan ahead so you are not rushing around to get it done last minute.

You may want to utilize a planner board and equipment stickers to document your activities. Before beginning your monthly preventative maintenance schedule, communicate with your manager so he/she can distribute resident letters. Your manager can help with notification and work orders for entering resident apartments.

Any time we enter a resident's apartment we are required to leave written notification. When conducting preventative maintenance, you can save time by writing one work order. Under work performed, write or type in "Changed A/C filters in buildings 6 – 10" and make copies for each occupied apartment. After completing the work, leave a copy of the work order in each occupied apartment in a visible area.

Maintenance cannot underestimate the role he/she plays in property management. On any give property maintenance is responsible for maintaining millions of dollar's worth of real estate. By definition, it is the job of maintenance to maintain the equipment and structures and the ground they stand on to prevent undue wear or deterioration to the equipment and structures.

The guidelines set forth in this section were drawn from industry standards and should be adhered to.

## PREVENTATIVE MAINTENANCE CHECKLIST

The Preventative Maintenance Checklist helps you organize your time and efforts in preventative maintenance. This is important as it will catch potential problems before they arise or become harder-to handle situations. Preventative maintenance is a very important part of your job and is taken very seriously by this company.

You should complete a preventative maintenance checklist monthly. A property calendar should include the due date of the Preventative Maintenance Schedule. Close communication with your Manager will eliminate hurried completion of this very important task.

## ENERGY CONSERVATION

In order to reduce operating costs, you should be prepared to be more energy and utility conscious.

- Vacant utility usage
- Domestic hot water utility usage
- Major mechanical usage
- Clubhouse utility usage
- Exterior plumbing
- Exterior lighting

If you cut back usage or improve the efficiency of your usage of utilities your property can save BIG.

## VACANT UTILITY USAGE

This is the area with the greatest potential savings and it should be the easiest usage to manage. Educate contractors and back charge the utility bill if they violate your utility usage program by leaving on all the lights and air conditioning after leaving the units. Educate your team members in proper usage. There is no reason for vacant utility usage to exceed the budgeted amount per unit.

Several procedures are:

- Turn off all breakers – except the refrigerator – upon leaving the unit. Set refrigerators and freezers to the warmest setting.

- If weather dictates, set the heater at 50°; a level which will prevent freezing, but will not waste energy. This should be done only if the outside temperatures are at 32° or below.

- Avoid faucet leaks. If you walk a unit after vacancy and find the faucets running or dripping, turn off the water supply to the angle stops or the main to that apartment. If you do not have this convenience, put in a service request to have the faucets repaired as soon as possible.

- Set guidelines for energy usage by your vendors and contractors. It is good policy to never set the A/C below 80° or the heater above 65° while working in a vacant apartment. The breakers should be turned off – except the refrigerator – before leaving the apartment.  Exception: If the carpets have just been shampooed, the carpet vendor may leave the HVAC (Fan Only) on until the carpet is dry.  This will prevent the carpet from souring.

- Make sure individual water heaters are off. Water heaters generally use 20% to 30% of an average utility bill.

- <u>You should mark all breakers.</u> Staff and contractors should be trained to selectively use breakers when in the unit and turn them back off when leaving.

- Cut down on light usage in vacant units; use lower wattage bulbs. Clean fixture lenses, bulbs, etc., at turn over. Dirty lenses and bulbs can waste 50% of the available light which in turn wastes 50% of the energy the property is paying for. Use 115 volt rated light bulbs for make readies. They are less expensive than the 130 volt long life bulbs.

## HOUSE LIGHTING

If the property pays for the house lighting.

- Photo cell systems should be used.  Exterior building lights should not be on during the day light hours.

- An evaluation should be made on the wattages of bulbs used in exterior lighting. Again, dirty lenses or diffusers should be cleaned thoroughly and lower wattage bulbs selected.

- You should use HPS (high pressure sodium) lighting for exterior lights. Par flood lights are not efficient.

## DOMESTIC HOT WATER

Another common energy wasting item is domestic hot water heaters. Normally, the main cause of energy wasting is the lack of routine maintenance to the burners and tanks. The main cause of this is the buildup of scale on the bottom of the heating vessel. For each 1/8" build-up of scale, 10% of a unit's efficiency is lost. To help save energy and prolong the life of these heaters you must:

- Remove cleaning port and flush out and remove all scale on the walls and bottom of the heating vessel at least once a year.  Follow the Preventative Maintenance Schedule.

- Insure proper air-gas mix at burners and adjust to proper out flame color (blue); clean any deposited soot from vessel, tubes and baffles.

Apartment Medic cost-saving tips are:

- Keep equipment rooms clean. Accumulated dust and grime on electric motors can cause them to work harder, less efficiently and shorten the life span.

- Keep motors oiled to improve efficiency and prolong life. Do not over-oil. This can be as damaging as no oil.

- Perform inspections on domestic hot water systems on a monthly basis and make repairs as noted during your inspection.

- Insure combustion air passageways are clean and allow free movement of air, insuring complete combustion of gas.

- Insulate exposed piping to boilers and hot water heaters. You lose 45 BTUs per hour, per linear foot on 1-1/2" pipe.

## MAJOR MECHANICAL

On communities with hydronic heating and cooling systems, a 10% slip in efficiency of the equipment can cost thousands of dollars in utility bills. Major equipment such as chillers, boilers, cooling towers, etc., should be maintained in prime condition.

Apartment Medic cost-saving tips are:

- Insure that equipment is properly lubricated at all times.

- Be sure to have an adequate water treatment program on-going for both the closed loop part of the system and open condensing cooling tower circuit. Insure that the boiler-condenser and evaporator tubes are clean and free from scale.

- Open drain valves on boilers periodically to flush out particles which have settled on the bottom of the boiler.  Follow the Preventative Maintenance Schedule.

- Insure that the boiler has an ambient temperature control installed. This automatically lowers the boiler's water temperature level as the outdoor (ambient) temperature rises. The payback in energy savings by installing an ambient temperature control is normally 1 to 3 months.

- Insure that the cooling towers are cleaned of all debris, i.e. algae, leaves, dirt, etc., to improve efficiency.
- Keep all equipment rooms clean. Dirt can lodge in motor air cooling vents, bearings, burners, etc., robbing the efficiency of the equipment and its life span.

- Insure that the boiler burners have the proper air-gas mix.

- Insure that the fire box on boilers is tight and free from rust and are containing the heat inside the boiler.

- Insure that all equipment is cycling properly. If not, notify the property manager.

- Insure combustion air passageways, grills, diffusers, screens, etc., are free from dust, dirt and obstructions to improve efficiency. Also, insure all fans and air moving equipment are operating properly.

- Insure water temperature on chillers and boilers is at the most economical setting for the size of equipment versus the number of units it supplies. In other words, don't have the chiller water temperature set at 40°F if 45°F will adequately cool the units.

- Change air filters in apartments regularly. This can cut energy usage drastically. Also insure the coils are clean.

- Keep up-to-date operating logs on major equipment. This will help spot equipment problems which can waste energy.

## CLUBHOUSE UTILITIES

Just a few energy basics are required to save money in this area.

- Turn off lights when leaving.

- Set back thermostats when leaving.

- Install ceiling fans and lower the thermostats.

- Insure that you have adequate weather stripping to protect against heating and cooling loss.

- Clean all light fixture lenses regularly.

- Use motion-controlled lights whenever possible in areas like the model, business center, public restrooms.

## EXTERIOR PLUMBING

Just a few basics are required to help reduce costs.

- Report leaks immediately.

- Do not allow sprinkler systems to run longer than necessary.

- Fix broken sprinkler heads immediately. A broken or missing sprinkler head can use as much water in 10 minutes as the entire sprinkler system uses in a day.

- Never allow water on concrete and driveways.

- Insure that the sprinkler system is metered separately from the domestic water supply.

- If applicable, winterize your system to prevent water waste during the spring start-up.

## RESIDENT SERVICES

After studying this section you will:

- Understand the importance of maintenance service to your residents
- Understand the purposes of the service request form
- Learn how to handle a service request

## THE IMPORTANCE OF SERVICE TO YOUR RESIDENTS

**Maintenance service is the most important function in resident services on any community.**

Your residents pay for service every time they pay their rent. If the resident is satisfied with the work you complete in his/her apartment they will feel better about writing that check out every month. Subsequently, if you do not take care of our residents, they will move and we will be left with a vacant apartment that will need to be made ready again. This means more work for everyone and more expense for your community. You directly affect the income for your property and your company!

Good policy is to complete service requests in 24 hours or less.

The service request form serves several purposes:

- It initiates the maintenance process.
- It allows the manager to track and follow up on requests for services.
- It records in the permanent record service performed.
- It is a tool for evaluating productivity.

The Apartment Maintenance Handbook by Eric Flynn

## THE SERVICE REQUEST PROCESS

All requests for service are to be handled in the following manner:

- All requests for repair are to be properly recorded.  Lock change requests must be in writing and completed by the end of that work day.

- It is good policy to complete each service request within 24 hours or less.

- When the work has been completed, the service request form should be completed in a clear and concise manner. The technician should sign the form, indicate the time in and time out of the apartment and summarize the work done

- **A copy for the resident should be left in a visible location in the resident's apartment. If the work cannot be completed due to a part needed or other circumstances, this should be noted on the work order copy left in the resident's apartment.**

- Return a copy to the office. All completed service request forms should be turned in to the manager _daily._

- After hour maintenance calls should be recorded as a service request.

## MAINTENANCE EMERGENCIES

It will be necessary to obtain the resident's phone number so that, prior to responding in person to an emergency call, maintenance personnel can make phone contact with the resident and determine the nature of the emergency. This will also help to ensure that the appropriate equipment and supplies are available.

<u>Maintenance Emergencies Defined</u>

- No heat or air conditioning when outside temperature is below 50° or above 85°
- Electrical failure of any nature
- Overflowing commode
- Stopped-up commode if only one is available
- Water problems (severe plumbing or roof leaks)
- Refrigerator malfunction
- No hot water
- Any unsecured entry or window
- Fire or electrical sparks

## SWIMMING POOL MAINTENANCE

After studying this section, you will:

- Know the steps in daily care of your swimming pool
- Understand basic pool maintenance
- Learn about different filter systems
- Understand the mechanics of pool filtration
- Learn how to control algae
- Learn about water chemistry and chemicals

The Apartment Maintenance Handbook by Eric Flynn

## SWIMMING POOL MAINTENANCE SCHEDULING

Swimming pools are an integral part of the total amenity package of your property. In order to assure the functional utility, the appeal and the well-being of pool users, it is crucial that proper operation and maintenance techniques be carried out.

It is essential that you, the Maintenance Technician, are familiar with the operational procedures relative to your own pool(s). Daily pool maintenance is a requirement that should not be taken lightly.

If you are not trained in the safety and care of pools, have your Manager schedule a class for you through a local organization. Your pool should be clean and pleasant places for our residents and guests.

## DAILY CARE

1. Perform daily maintenance to your pool, which in apartment communities is required throughout the day. Ideally your pool water should be crystal clear. You should be able to distinguish the difference between a dime and a nickel lying in the deepest part of the pool.

2. Debris such as leaves, dirt, etc. should be removed daily or as soon as they accumulate.

3. The pool tile should be scrubbed clean as often as necessary to remove sun tanning oil and deposits. Failure to do this can result in an unsightly lime deposit which can be very difficult to remove.

4. During periods of heavy use the pool deck and furniture should be hosed down regularly. Furniture should be arranged on a daily basis.

5. A detailed schematic of your pool valve operation must be kept in a Swimming Pool Log.

## BASIC POOL MAINTENANCE

The basic pool maintenance below is to be completed daily and more often during early Spring and Fall when there is a heavy fall-out from trees and bushes.

1. Manually skim the pool surface with the leaf skimmer. Ensure your leaf skimmer has a long enough handle to reach to the pool's center while standing on the pool deck.

2. Brush down the walls and tile with a stiff-bristled tile brush and a wall brush.

3. Clean the skimmer basket and the hair lint strainer. Remove the skimmer basket and the pump's hair lint strainer. Remove debris that has collected and replace both. Failure to keep baskets clean will result in reduced circulation, introduction of air to the system and possible loss of the circulating prime.

4. Vacuum the Pool Bottom

**Step 1**     The pool needs to be vacuumed daily. It should be brushed thoroughly before beginning to vacuum. This will break loose any crust which the vacuum may not be strong enough to pick up. Also, if there are any leaves or loose objects of any type left in the pool, they should be dipped out in advance. Do not vacuum any objects into the system that might get stopped in the line such as toys, clothes, pins, etc.

**Step 2**     Be sure the filtering mechanism is in proper operational condition before starting to vacuum. Backwash, if necessary, and clean the pump basket.

**Step 3**     Make sure the valves on the skimmer lines leading to the filtration system are open and then close the valves on the main drain lines leading to the bottom of the pool. This has the effect of putting all pressure on the skimmer lines.

**Step 4**     Go to your pool deck and close off all skimmers from which you do not intend to vacuum at the moment. This is done by closing the float valve beneath the basket in the skimmers to the OFF position. Make sure they are tight and thoroughly closed.

**Step 5**     You are now ready to begin to vacuum from the skimmer suction line you plan to use. You may test to see if you have proper vacuum on this skimmer by putting your fingers down into the drain hole at the bottom of the skimmer to feel the vacuum. Connect the vacuum head to your vacuum hose and then put the remaining hose on the pool deck. Lead the hose into the water, hand over hand, until reaching the other end of the hose. Ease this end of the hose through the intake of the skimmer from the pool and into the drain hole of the skimmer. Do not place the hose over the top of the pool deck and down into the drain hole of the skimmer. Suction should hold the hose in position. The objective of feeding the hose into the water is to allow it to fill with water, minimizing the amount of air in the hose.

**Step 6**     Vacuum the pool using a back-and-forth motion to cover the entire pool floor and wall area. Be sure to watch the pressure gauge while vacuuming as it may be necessary to backwash the pool filter during the vacuum process. After vacuuming, backwash filters to dispose of dirt and debris.

## FILTER SYSTEMS

While chlorine or other disinfectants tend to clean the water "biologically," they cannot clean it physically. Physically clean water is water that is free from particulate matter such as suspended particles, dirt and dust. Physically clean water is obtained by pumping the water from the pool through a filter to remove solid particles.

Whether your filter is sand or diatomaceous earth they both work with the same principles. When water is forced through either media some particles of suspended matter in the water will cling to the grains of the media and others will be trapped in the spaces between them. As the spaces or voids between the grains become clogged with dirt it becomes increasingly difficult to force water through. Either the force used to move the water will have to be increased or the flow will decrease. When the flow has decreased sufficiently, the filter will require backwashing, which basically pushes the water in the opposite direction than the trapped particles entered.

**High rate sand filters** consist of a closed tank (either fiberglass or stainless steel), an upper distribution system, sand and a lower collection manifold. The collection manifold is designed so that it retains the filter media but allows water to pass freely.

- High rate sand filters operate at a flow rate up to 20 gallons per minute per square foot. In the basic operation of this type of filter, water enters from the pump through the upper distribution system which spreads the flow evenly over the sand. The surface of the sand collects suspended matter until a mat of filtered dirt is developed which creates a slightly increased pressure. This pressure increases forces these collected solids into the filter media, leaving the surface clean to repeat the process. As the filter run progresses the dirt partially fills the voids between sand grains and, in turn, traps even smaller particles. This is repeated continuously until depth reaches about 10". At that time backwashing is necessary. Backwashing reverses the direction of water flow and the sand bed expands causing the sand grains to rub together releasing the dirt to be carried as waste through the upper distribution arms. The thorough mixing of the sand grains during the backwash process prevents the layering of sand grains by sizes which would limit effectiveness.

- It has been found most economical to backwash at pressure increase of 10 to 15 pounds because the dirt penetration at that level will be at 6" to 10" into the sand. For that reason, a depth of sand of about 12" over the lower collection manifold is required. A filter should be backwashed until the existing water runs clear.

- Backwashing with dirty pool water is not recommended because it can clog the orifices in the lower distribution system. This will cause uneven filter flow. If the condition does not correct itself it may be necessary to remove the sand and physically clean the under-drains. Using the filter backwash cycle to drain a pool will almost surely result in this problem.

**Diatomaceous earth filters** are sometimes called diatomite or abbreviated as D.E. D.E. is composed of fossil remains of aquatic plants which average less than 1/1000 of an inch in size. Each tiny fossil is porous, containing minute passages which can only be measured in microns. Water passes through and around these grains, but the openings are so small that a layer only 1/8 of an inch thick is equivalent to a filter bed of sand 2 feet in depth. These filters are designed to operate from 1 to 2.6 grams per minute per square foot of filter surface.

The Apartment Maintenance Handbook by Eric Flynn

There are two basic types of D.E. filters: a pressure D.E. filter which uses a closed tank and a vacuum D.E. filter which uses an open tank or pit. Pressure D.E. filter tanks are normally made of stainless steel. Vacuum types may be made of concrete, steel, aluminum or fiberglass. These tanks contain filter elements which are closely woven screens of stainless steel, metal or synthetic fabrics such as Dacron, nylon or polyethylene. The screens are supported on metal or plastic frames or grids to keep them rigid. These elements vary greatly in size and shape. They may be cylindrical, flat, disc-shaped, flat sheets or thin curved sheets in concentric circles.

The basic operation of a D.E. filter should be as follows. The filter must be isolated from the pool water by closing the valves leading from the pool to the filter and from the filter to the pool. The recycling valve must be opened allowing the water from the filter to be cycled directly back to the pump and back into the filter again. Many properties that have D.E. filters do not have this recycling valve set up, which does not allow you to properly charge the D.E. filter.

The D.E. filter should always be charged with clean water; when the filter is full recycling begins. An amount of D.E. equal to about 2 ounces per square foot of filter surface area is added through a feeder called a "pre-coat pot," or added directly to the filter by hand if the tank is the open vacuum type. It is helpful to mix the D.E. with water prior to adding. As water passes through the filter the larger diatomite particles are trapped on the screen allowing the smaller diatomite particles to pass through. As the water is recycled the smaller particles are caught by the larger particles. This process goes on until the water that is being recycled runs clear. This process is called "pre-coating" and results in a smooth, even layer of diatomite on the elements of about 1/16 of an inch. The return line to the pool is either pushed or pulled through the filter elements.

After pre-coating is performed the pool supply and return valves are opened. The recycling or bypass valve is closed and the filter is ready for operation. The D.E. filter then works similar to the sand filter in that suspended particles are trapped by the diatomite as water passes through, progressively trapping even smaller particles until the rate of flow decreases and the pressure or vacuum increases. Most pressure type D.E. filters can be operated to pressures of 35 to 40 lbs., while vacuum D.E. filters should be cleaned when the vacuum gauge shows about 10" to 12" of mercury.
Because D.E. filters are highly efficient, they can clog quite rapidly. The rate at which this clogging occurs can be slowed down somewhat by introducing a small amount of additional D.E. during the filter run. This additional layer mixes with the pre-coat layer and the dirt already trapped and keeps the filter layer porous. This process is called "slurry feeding" or "body feeding." With the amount of use a typical apartment pool experiences this process can be used to your advantage.

When the filter no longer responds to slurry feeding it is necessary to clean it. This may be accomplished by many methods depending on the size of your filter. It may be reverse flow or a momentary surge of reverse flow. Some are cleaned by flexing the element in the tank or by rotating the entire element in the tank by a crank. Most vacuum style filters are cleaned by a garden hose.

Whatever the cleaning process is it begins by first turning the pump off. The valves leading from the pool and to the pool are closed and the recycling valve is opened. When the pump is turned off the pressure holding the diatomite to the filter screen is released and it loosens immediately, providing it is not saturated with oil and is a clay consistency. The D.E. and dirt falls to the bottom of the tank and is washed to waste through the backwash cycle. When the tank is cleaned the pre-coat process is repeated.

Whenever the pump is stopped – even momentarily – the filter cake loosens, shifts and may drop from the elements. Restarting the filter without backwashing causes dirt to come in direct contact with the filter elements, which may clog them. If the elements are clogged, or partially clogged in areas, an adequate coating of D.E. is not possible and the filter will not operate with total coverage. This, in turn, will overload other areas of the elements, compacting dirt and particles into them. It is for this reason that recycling valve setups should be installed. A D.E. filter is normally judged to need cleaning when the pool water is dirty. D.E. filters should always be pre-coated with a clean water supply.

Another advantage of having the recycle valve is that if the filters become clogged with sun tanning oil, it can usually be removed by adding a generous amount of low sudsing detergent, recycling it through the filters for 2 to 3 hours, then backwashing the detergent mixture to waste.

On some occasions the filter will become so clogged that the only solution is to break down the filter, clean the elements by hand and hose them down or scrub them clean prior to reassembly and precoating.

# THE MECHANICS OF POOL FILTRATION

While all pools are not the same, most of them will work along the following principle:

- The pool system is a closed line water pressure system. There should be no air infiltrating into the pressure system at any point and all lines should be totally filled with water at all times. If you understand this beginning principle, then you will be on your way to understanding pool mechanics.

- No changes in pool operations from one procedure to another (i.e. from normal filtration to backwashing) should be made without closing off the motors. If a person attempts to go from one procedure to the other without first turning off the motors, it has the same effect as trying to shift an automobile from a forward gear to reverse without first stopping the vehicle and going through neutral.

- There is a certain number of pounds of pressure developed by the water in the closed line system. Any great variance in the pressure gauge governing this system – either less pressure or more pressure – indicates some malfunction in the system. Typically an increase in pressure will indicate the need to backwash the pool.

**Backwashing (Cleaning the pool filter system):**

**Step 1**  Turn off the motors. Turn the filtration system dial valve to OFF. Close all suction valves incoming from the pool. These are generally the valves on the water line which bring unclean water to the filtering system from the drain or drains on the bottom of the pool and from the skimmer drains on the deck of the pool. If your pool has a separate chlorination system which uses stick chlorine it is necessary to cut off the chlorination valves admitting chlorine into the system. After having cut off the above-mentioned valves, remove the pump strainer basket, clean thoroughly and replace. After replacing the pump strainer lid you are then ready to reopen the suction valves. Never open the suction valves without first replacing the lid because air will get into the line, violating the first principle of the closed water pressure system.

**Step 2**  Close the air relief valve. In normal operation this small valve is ordinarily in a vertical position. Turn the dial valve from the OFF position to BACKWASH. You are now ready to turn the motor back ON. The system should be run in this backwash position from 5 to 7 minutes, depending on the size of the pool. Some pool filtration systems are furnished with a sight glass for viewing the backwashing procedure. When backwashing has been accomplished the water in the sight glass clears up and loses its cloudy appearance. After allowing ample time for backwashing, turn the motor OFF again.

**Step 3**  Turn the dial valve from the backwash position to filter-to-waste position. In this position all the debris and waste that was accumulated during the backwash procedure will now be washed into the sewer line. After placing the dial valve in the filter-to-waste position, turn the motor ON for approximately 1 minute which will accomplish this step. Then turn the motor OFF again.

**Step 4**   <u>Resume normal operating procedure</u>. This is done by turning the dial valve to the filter position and cutting the motors back ON. Be sure to return the air-release valve to the vertical position so that it will be in position for ejection of air that may have gained its way into the system through some abnormal procedure or malfunction.

**"Do's" and "Don'ts" Pertaining to Backwashing:**

DO:   Clean all skimmer baskets before backwashing.

Clean the pump basket any time the gauges indicate higher than normal pressure.

Most filter gauges have a red hand on the gauge which is set in a rigid position. The black hand on the gauge indicates the pressure within the line. When the black hand catches up with or approaches the red hand it is time to backwash.

DON'T:   Backwash with the vacuum hose in the skimmer.
Never move the dial valve while the motor is running.

**NOTE:**   Sometimes the pump will lose its prime during the above procedures. If this should happen, be sure to cut off the pump motors as the motors are water lubricated and will rapidly deteriorate if they are on without water being pumped through the system. Remove the basket lid and after the suction valves are turned off (as in Step 1 above) fill the pump line from the basket to the suction valves with water. Put the lid back on before reopening suction valves. (If this is not done, air will get in the line.) After opening the suction valves, quickly turn the dial valves to the filter position and turn motor on immediately. This should re-prime the pump.

## ALGAE CONTROL

Algae are small microscopic organisms which possess an internal green pigment called chlorophyll. These organisms are the normal inhabitants of surface waters and are encountered in every water supply that is exposed to sunlight. If ideal conditions for their growth exist in a water supply, it is possible to develop a thriving algae population within 24 hours. Furthermore, if water contains considerable dissolved minerals and other suspended matter, the algae has nutrients for its growth and the growth of other microscopic aquatic life.

The problem with algae control is a serious and ever-present one in swimming pools. The presence of even small numbers of algae in swimming pools or other water supplies tends to clog filters and impart disagreeable odors and tastes to the water. Furthermore, algae can interfere with the efficiency and effectiveness of chlorine, iodine and bromine – common disinfectants used in swimming pools.

Once algae have developed in a swimming pool, particularly the so-called "wall-clinging" types, even super-chlorination of the water (10 ppm free available chlorine) cannot destroy the algae mats which often form on the sides and bottoms of the pools. Chlorine can only be effective as an algistat to prevent the growth and development of some algae if it is present in a pool at all times in concentrations of 1 ppm; but is not an effective algicide in controlling and killing black algae, which cause the biggest problems in swimming pools.

Algae are not usually harmful to swimmers. But they are objectionable. And they can cause personal hazard – particularly the slimy type which make the pool bottom slippery. Discoloring the plaster or bottom, they obscure the pool and make it hard to see objects on the bottom. From an aesthetic standpoint a pool with algae appears unsightly and dirty. Because so many strains of algae are immune to disinfectants present in the pool, special treatment with chemical algicides is necessary at all times to control them.

These plant forms are brought into the pool by the wind and with fresh make-up water. If uncontrolled, they will grow abundantly in the presence of sunlight. They are found in the free floating and clinging varieties. The clinging type will adhere itself into pores and crevices on the pool floor and walls and is more resistant to treatment. Algae are nature's way of oxidizing organic waste material. From the decomposing of this waste material carbon dioxide ($CO_2$) is released and it is the $CO_2$ that is necessary for algae to live.

## Objectionable Features of Algae

- <u>Chlorine demand</u>. Since they are organic in nature, algae will create a high chlorine demand. Once they have a hold in the pool, maintenance of a chlorine residual is difficult.

- <u>Water turbidity</u>. Increased turbidity in the pool due to algae is not only aesthetically objectionable, but it creates a hazard to proper swimmer supervision.

- <u>Slipping</u>. Algae growth increases the chance of pool accidents due to slipping on pool bottoms, sides, walkways and ladders.

- <u>Effect on bacterial growth</u>. In addition to protecting bacteria from the effects of chlorine by creating a high chlorine demand themselves, algae also actually may foster bacterial growth.

## Detecting Algae Growth Early

As a plant, algae require carbon dioxide in order to manufacture food. In the process of taking carbon dioxide out of water, there is a definite increase in the pH. A radical jump in pH (from 7.5 to 8.0, for example) over a period of several hours will indicate growth before there is any visible growth in the water.

## Algicides and Special Anti-Algae Chemical Guidelines

To prevent the development of particularly stubborn cases of pool algae and to kill algae growth already present in the pool, it is necessary to regularly add an algicide to the pool water.

Algicides are chemical compounds or formulations specifically designed to prevent its growth and to kill existing algae in the pool. Algicides may be obtained from the pool supplier. Effective algicides for swimming pools should:

- be effective against all strains of algae found in swimming pools, especially the more resistant Black Algae.

- be completely independent of chlorine treatment and should not interfere with the effectiveness of chlorine as a disinfectant by rendering it inactive.

- remain active at least during the periods between treatments as given by the manufacturer.

The Apartment Maintenance Handbook by Eric Flynn

- have no adverse effect on water such as clouding, excessive foaming, undesirable odor, taste, etc.

- be of low toxicity at use levels so as not to cause adverse effects on the health of swimmers.

- not be absorbed or be destroyed by the filter media.

- not precipitate out in the water or react with natural occurring ingredients or with chemicals added to the water.

- be easy and economical to use.

## Methods of Algae Control

- <u>Routine chlorination</u>. The maintenance of chlorine-free residual in the pool at all times will prevent the start of algae troubles.

- <u>Pool shading</u>. Since algae need sunlight for growth, shaded pools will tend to have less growth, but not prevent it.

- <u>Temperature</u>. When the pool water is below 80° F, algae is minimized.

## The Application of Copper Sulfate

- <u>Shock Treatment</u>. Dissolve copper sulfate crystals before adding to the pool. A treatment dose of 5 pounds per million gallons of pool water can be introduced by putting crystals into a porous bag and moving it through the pool water, or into a skimmer or hair/lint strainer.

- <u>Maintenance Dosing</u>.    Pools that experience continuous algae difficulties due to some uncontrollable factor may practice preventative application of copper sulfate. This may be done by introducing an initial dose of 0.5 ppm and maintaining a 0.3 to 0.5 ppm level by dosing every 5 to 7 days.

## Difficulties with Copper Sulfate

- <u>Effect of hard water</u>. The effective portion of the copper compound is rendered ineffective by alkaline carbonate.

- <u>Effect on swimmers</u>. The compound may discolor swimsuits and hair. Excessive amounts of copper sulfate are very drying to mucous membranes.

- <u>Production of an inky precipitate</u>. Hydrogen sulfide is present in the water. This causes a precipitate of copper sulfide.

## Application of Quatenary Ammonium Compounds

Quatenary ammonium compounds are not intended as a substitute for a disinfecting agent. However, they will permit the disinfectant to have a greater effect in attacking algae because of the lowered surface tension of the pool water. The usual dose is 1 gallon per 50,000 gallons of water initially, and subsequent dosages of 1 quart per 50,000 gallons every 6 days.

## Super-Chlorination

One of the most effective treatments is the development of a 1 ppm free chlorine residual in the pool during non-swimming hours.

Excessively high residuals may be reduced to permit swimming by adding sodium thiosulfate to the water at the rate of 1.0 to 1.55 ppm for each 1.0 ppm of residual chlorine being removed.

## Pool Scrubbing

As a last resort, the pool may be drained, and the bottom and sides scrubbed with a 5% hypochlorite slurry or copper sulfate solution to remove tenacious algae growths. Scrubbing will also remove any dead algae that have turned black and are clinging to the walls.

## Pool Paints

A durable, smooth surface created by painting with rubber-based, waterproof, enamel paint will resist the intrusion of clinging algae. Consult Manufacturer's Specifications regarding proper procedures for applying pool paints.

## WATER CHEMISTRY AND CHEMICALS

### The Use of Pool Chemicals

Complete sanitation of pool water requires chemicals that will control bacteria, algae and fungi quickly and surely. These contaminants are brought into the water by swimmers, air, rain, or may already be in the water. They contribute to undesirable pools and will result in dirty or unsightly water. Although a good filtration system is necessary for any pool, no filtration system alone is capable of eliminating all contaminants. Certain chemicals must be added to the swimming pool to control contamination.

- <u>Chlorination</u>. There are several types of chlorination systems available. Most of the more recent pools use the Widget type stick chlorination while many of the older pools require the use of powdered chlorine. **Do not mix 99% chlorine sticks with 65% granular calcium hypochlorite as an explosion may result.** Regardless of the type of chlorination system, the primary purpose of chlorine is to protect swimmers from germ contamination. When used in proper quantities, chlorine will kill bacterial germs which are harmful to the human body. Algae are vegetation which, in itself, is not harmful. Algae does, however, harbor bacteria. Algae will soak up or eat the chlorine content, sometimes creating an imbalance in the swimming pool. To combat algae formation, administer an overdose of chlorine, or in pool terminology "shock" the pool with chlorine. If this does not help curb the growth of algae, many pool people use copper sulfate. Copper sulfate is to be administered only by pool experts.

- <u>Maintaining a "residual" of disinfectant</u>. From the very first day the pool is filled, its purity must be guarded (and maintained) by a chemical disinfectant. Generally, some purifying chemical, whether chlorine, bromine or iodine, must be maintained in the pool water and enough of it must reside there to kill disease carrying bacteria brought into the water by swimmers.

  The amount of chemical residual which must be present in pool water is expressed as "ppm," or parts per million. (The same quantitative measure is used to express the amount of any other chemical added or present in pool water.)

  Chlorine is the most widely used and acceptable disinfectant for swimming pools. When chlorine is used as a disinfectant, 0.6 to 1.0 of "free residual chlorine" MUST – at all times – be present in order to kill bacteria and maintain the water's purity. Less free residual than 1.0 ppm will fail to kill bacteria. **NOTE: These recommended concentrations apply to chlorine only and do not reflect the concentrations required when using other types of disinfectants.**

  Critical though this residual is for pool purity, it is a very small amount of chemical. Less than 1 drop of chlorine in every 1,000,000 drops of pool water is enough to disinfect, providing the chemical is 100% active.

### Factors affecting Longevity of Disinfectant Residuals

The following is a list of the most common factors affecting the in-pool longevity of chlorine and other disinfectants.

- Bathing Load – the number of swimmers who use the pool. The greater the number of swimmers, the more disinfectant is used up.

The Apartment Maintenance Handbook by Eric Flynn

- Sunlight – the greater the sun's intensity, the faster the dissipation of disinfectant residual.

- Water Temperature – the warmer the pool's temperature, the shorter the life of most chemicals used as disinfectants.


- Winds and Rain – dust, bacteria, algae, spores and other debris are carried into the pool, overworking chemical disinfectant and reducing their power to sanitize.

- pH Balance – the higher the pH of the pool water, the slower acting most pool disinfectants are. More disinfectants must usually be added to maintain the proper bacteria-killing residual. **The ideal pH range for pool water is 7.2 to 7.6.**

- Total Alkalinity – the amount of alkaline salts present in pool water. If total alkalinity is low (below 80 to 100 ppm) pH will fluctuate widely and the pool plaster may etch. If too high, it will tend to maintain pH at a higher than desired level and cause scale and cloudy water.

**Types of Swimming Pool Disinfectants**

There are basically 3 chemicals (chlorine, bromine and iodine) now used successfully to disinfect swimming pool water. Whatever disinfectant is used, **it is IMPORTANT to use the disinfectant properly, as recommended by the manufacturer. It is also important to test pool water with the appropriate test kit:** chlorine, pH, total alkalinity or others as recommended by the manufacturer.

- <u>Chlorine as a disinfectant</u>. Chlorine has been used for many years and recognized by public agencies and engineering groups as an effective agent to disinfect water for drinking or recreational (swimming) purposes.

    Chlorine Gas – (chemically, "basic elemental chlorine") Although chlorine gas is used to purify some large (municipal or club) pools it is not recommended by most producers for residential or home use except under carefully controlled conditions. Since it is a gas – and a potentially dangerous one – it must be contained in a pressure tank. Its use requires an automatic feeder – called a chlorinator – which adjusts the dosage of gaseous chlorine fed to the pool.

    Liquid Chlorine – (chemically, "sodium hypochlorite") Liquid chlorine is available in various concentrations from 5 ¼% to 14% available chlorine by weight. Due to its limited stability in the higher concentrations, supplies should be fresh and used without prolonged storage. To improve its stability, manufacturers add alkali (often caustic soda) to liquid chlorines. Thus, liquid chlorine's inherent basic character tends to raise the pH of pool water (turn pool water more and more alkaline). To neutralize this increasing alkalinity, it may be necessary to periodically add an alkalineutralizer such as muriatic acid or sodium bisulfate to the water.

    Calcium Hypochlorite – This dry, soluble form of chlorine is available in granular or tablet form and usually contains about 50% to 70% available chlorine. In using calcium hypochlorite as a disinfectant, care must be taken in balancing the pool's water to the recommended pH of 7.2 to 7.6. As with the liquid sodium hypochlorite, the excess alkalinity in calcium hypochlorite often requires use of an acid (muriatic or sodium bisulfate) to neutralize the alkalinity and maintain pool water balance at the recommended pH.

Lithium Hypochlorite – This is also a dry, stable form of chlorine available as free flowing granules and contains 35% available chlorine. It is less alkaline than calcium hypochlorite and, therefore, less adjustment of pH of the water is required when this compound is used as a disinfectant. However, as is the case for any disinfectant, be sure to adjust the pH of the pool before beginning regular care of the pool.

Chlorinated Iso Cyanurate (Tri-Chlor) – This dry, stable organic chlorine compound has demonstrated its effectiveness as a disinfectant. One of its chief advantages is longer stability (thus longer life under most conditions) in pool water. Iso cyanurates differ, both chemically and physically, from the inorganic types of disinfectants and should be used only according to the manufacturer's recommendations. Proper pH level for this sanitizer is 7.2 to 7.6.

- <u>Bromine as a disinfectant</u>.

Liquid Bromine – Elemental bromine is a very heavy liquid with bactericidal properties similar to chlorine. In routine pool usage it requires about twice as much bromine by weight to maintain a disinfecting residual in pool water compared to chlorine. Extreme care in handling liquid bromine is necessary as it may cause severe burns if spilled on the body. At room temperature bromine vaporizes readily to release irritating fumes. Mechanical feeding equipment is available.

Dry (stick-type) Bromine – Dry bromine in stick form can be handled with the same ease as powdered chlorine and does not cause the relative changes in pH as the chlorine products. Use it only as directed by the manufacturer.

- <u>Iodine as a disinfectant</u>. Iodine or iodine compounds are used as a pool water disinfectant. Carefully controlled water balance (alkalinity and pH) is necessary. Use only as directed by the manufacturer.

Iodine, another member of the halogen family, is related to bromine and chlorine. As an element it normally exists as a solid (or crystals) and must be combined with something else before becoming soluble in water. Compounds containing iodine (iodides) – usually potassium – are used with a suitable activating agent such as hypochlorite. These compounds will release elemental iodine in the pool water to serve as a disinfectant. Carefully controlled water balance is essential when using iodine compounds.

**Adding Chemical Disinfectants**

To maintain the pool's bacteria-killing residual, disinfectant chemicals may be added by hand, automatically or by a chemical feeder. Feeders may be adjusted to increase or decrease the feed rate of disinfectant, depending on the chemical demand of the pool. (If the pool does not have an automatic chemical feeder the chemicals must be added by hand.)

- <u>Liquid disinfectants</u>. Liquid disinfectants are simply poured into pool water. Begin at the deep end. Move completely around the pool, pouring the disinfectant to distribute it throughout the pool. **NOTE: avoid contact with eyes, skin or clothing.** Wear protective eye wear.

- <u>Granular or tablet form disinfectants</u>. Dry disinfectants should likewise be evenly distributed in pool water. Sometimes disinfectant tablets are bagged and hung in the water at various spots near the deeper end. Sometimes powdered disinfectants are "sowed," much like one would sow grass seed. This process merely involves walking around the pool's edge sowing the water with the chemical. Some dry disinfectants tend to cause the pool water to become slightly cloudy for a short time after application. Wear protective eye wear.

**Test the Water for Disinfectant Residual**

A simple test kit (available from your pool supplier) permits proper testing for disinfectant residual. If the test kit indicates that pool water contains too little residual, it will be necessary to add enough disinfectant to restore the proper and recommended residual level. Test kits are available for testing chlorine, bromine or iodine residuals.

It is only necessary to take a small sample of pool water as directed and a measured amount of the color-reacting chemical supplied with the kit. Compare the water sample's resultant color with a set of standard colors in the kit. The kit's standard colors indicate the amount of residual in the pool. As an example: to test for chlorine residual, take a sample of pool water in the test tube that comes with the kit, add the suggested amount of test chemical, mix the sample well and – depending on the water's residual – a color will develop. The lower the chlorine content, the paler the color of the sample; the higher the chlorine content, the deeper the color. Compare the sample's color to the standard color

samples in the kit. Each standard sample is marked with the amount of residual the sample represents. If the test tube's color matches the standard sample labeled – between 0.6 and 1.0 ppm – then the pool water has the proper residual and no new chemical needs to be added. If, on the other hand, color sample comparison indicates too little chlorine, disinfectant must be added until the proper residual is obtained for the pool water.

- Cyanuric Acid. To help maintain a pool's ability to hold chlorine, cyanuric acid should be added as needed. This is also referred to as "balancing" a pool's water. Most pool stores will perform the cyanuric test for you, but will not volunteer the fact that the pool should be balanced, simply because a balanced pool will use less chlorine so they will sell less.

This test should be performed several times per season or whenever significant amounts of make-up water is added to the pool. In areas where pools are drained down for the winter, it is extremely important that the pool be balanced when it is initially filled. Many of the tri-chlor compounds have, as part of their formula, stabilizing compounds. It is still important that the water be balanced to begin with.

Cyanuric acid is widely used as a stabilizing agent for chlorine. It is introduced directly into the pool to produce a concentration of 30 to 50 ppm and the concentration must be checked occasionally to insure its retention within recommended limits. The suggested upper limit is 100 ppm.

Test kits are available for checking cyanuric acid concentration. They contain a melamine solution which makes a pool water sample turbid if it contains cyanuric acid. The turbid solution is poured into a vial containing a black disc in the bottom. The depth of the solution required to completely obscure the disc is calibrated in ppm of cyanurate and is read directly from the vial.

The ideal pH level for pool water is between 7.2 and 7.6. Water that is neutral – that is neither basic nor acidic – has a pH value of 7.0. This is midpoint on the 0 to 14 pH scale. Pool water above 7.0 pH is alkaline; below 7.0 pH pool water is acidic. The higher up the pH scale the pool water tests, the more alkaline it is; the lower down the pH scale pool water tests, the more acidic it is.

Maintaining the pool water very slightly on the alkaline side (7.2 to 7.6 pH) is important for a number of reasons. When pool water is too alkaline (above 8.0 pH) disinfecting chemicals work more slowly. They may not do their proper killing job even though tests of the water may indicate a proper residual. Also, scale may form on or in the pool equipment and piping. On the other hand, if pool water becomes acidic, it irritates the eyes, corrodes equipment and piping and the pool interior surface stains.

Correcting the pH of pool water is not difficult. To test for pH water balance, take another sample of pool water in a clean and separate test tube (also supplied with the kit). This time it is necessary to add a measured amount of a different test chemical, Phenol Red. If the pool's water is too acidic the water in the test tube turns yellow; if too alkaline the water turns red. Comparing the test tube's color with the standard kit color samples indicates whether the pool water is acidic or alkaline and to what degree. If the pool water's pH varies up or down the kit's pH scale from the recommended 7.2 to 7.6 pH, it will be necessary to add to the pool water enough acid or alkali chemical to restore the pH to the recommended and proper level. Since a high chlorine residual in the pool affects the water's pH, for more accurate measurement of the water's acid-alkaline balance, take the pH test when the chlorine residual is low, before adding disinfectant. **NOTE: Do not hold a finger over the top of the test tube while mixing. Body acid can cause a false test reading. Stopper the tube and mix by moving the test tube in a circular motion.**

If the test kit indicates that pool water has too high a pH, simply use a chemical designed to lower the water's pH. If tests show pool water to have too low pH, use a chemical that neutralizes the acidity and raises the pH.

### Common Chemicals that Raise and Lower pH

A number of water-balancing chemicals are available from pool suppliers. Some chemicals (highly basic) raise the pH level of pool water. Others (acidic chemicals) lower the pH.

- Soda Ash – RAISES pH. This cousin of common baking soda is among the least expensive and easiest to use of acid-neutralizing pool chemicals. Administer soda ash by walking around the pool sowing. It is also available in block form.

- Muriatic Acid and Sodium Bisulfate – LOWER pH. Commercial strength muriatic acid (available at most pool suppliers) is about 20% hydrochloric acid. No more than one pint of muriatic acid should be added to every 5,000 gallons of pool water at one time to reduce alkalinity and to re-establish the pool water's pH balance of 7.2 to 7.6.

Acid should be added judiciously. Available from the pool dealer is a special acid demand test kit which tells precisely how much acid should be added to lower pool water's pH. Whether use is made of an acid demand test kit or merely the addition of acid until the pH test kit shows the correct pool water balance, never add more than 1 pint of acid in a single dose. If the pH is still above 7.6, add another pint of acid. Continue this treatment until the pH is between 7.2 and 7.6.

If using an acid demand test kit which, for example, indicates that a quart of acid should be added, add 1 pint, allow it to circulate throughout the pool for 30 minutes to an hour, test again, then add the second recommended pint if tests indicate acid demand. Repeat as needed.

The Apartment Maintenance Handbook by Eric Flynn

**HANDLE MURIATIC ACID, AS ANY ACID, WITH CARE. IF THE ACID SPILLS ON SKIN OR CLOTHING, WASH IT OFF IMMEDIATELY.** Wear protective eye wear.

**Total Alkalinity and What It Means**

Occasionally pool water should also be tested for "total alkalinity." Total alkalinity is a measurement of the total amount of alkaline chemicals in the water. It refers to the degree of resistance to pH change of pool water or its "buffering" capacity. The proper alkalinity level is usually between 80 to 100 ppm.

- Low alkalinity waters make pH control difficult because of lack of buffering capacity (poor resistance to pH change.) Alkalinity must be increased in these waters to offset the possibility of the pool water reverting to acid. A level of pH below 7.0 can cause swimmer discomfort, corrosion of metal pool parts and bleaching of plaster pools. A rule for adding alkalinity is that 1 ½ pounds of sodium bicarbonate (baking soda) will raise the alkalinity of 10,000 gallons of water by 10 ppm.

- Many waters in the United States are of high alkalinity and high pH. To get these waters into the swimming pool comfort zone, it is necessary to destroy a portion of the alkalinity so the pH can be lowered. This can be accomplished by addition of muriatic acid or sodium bisulfate. The amount of acid required is referred to as acid demand. These tests are simple to do and the acid demand test kit mentioned previously provides complete information on the amount of acid required. In addition to the high pH and resulting poor chlorine residual efficiency, high pH and alkalinity can result in scale formation and a cloudy pool. To measure total alkalinity a total alkalinity test kit is used. Kits are available from pool suppliers.

**Pool Service Log Report**

Records of pool operation are required to monitor day-to-day chemical levels and other pertinent information. **The Pool Service Log must be maintained daily throughout the year.**

# GENERAL RULES REGARDING THE USE OF CHEMICALS

- Do not try to be a "know-it-all." Read directions carefully for all chemicals that are to be used.

- Do not overdose. Measure exact amounts. Pool chemicals – like medicine – should be used in specified amounts. Too much can cause irritating side effects.

- Do not guess. Take time to learn to use a test kit. Be sure to replace reagents (test fluids) each season to assure accuracy.

- Establish a routine for testing and treatment. A few minutes every day – or every other day – can make the job easy and assure that the pool is in tip-top shape.

- Do not mix 99% chlorine (tri-chlor) with 65% chlorine (calcium hypochloritic) – **an explosion could result.** If you are switching between these two types, all of the old type of chlorine must be out of the system, i.e. chlorinators, filters, water, etc.

- Wear protective eye wear every time you prepare and add chemicals to the pool.

## PURPOSE OF HAZARD COMMUNICATION PROGRAM

The purpose of the Written Hazard Communication Program is to describe the methods used to implement the Hazard Communication Program. This document outlines how each of the requirements set forth in the OSHA Hazard Communication Standard (HCS) 29 CRF 1910.1200 should be met at your facility.

## CONTAINER LABELING

You are responsible for ensuring labeling of onsite containers.

A.  Each container of hazardous material at this property received from an outside supplier should be clearly labeled with:

- Identity of hazardous chemical(s)
- Appropriate hazard warnings
- Name and address of the manufacturer

B.  Each non-empty container of hazardous materials on the property, including mixing tanks, storage tanks, drums, bags, bottles and boxes will have a label attached to it.

C.  Labels provided by vendors on incoming containers will not be defaced or removed. DO NOT accept shipments of hazardous material without proper labeling. Any containers of hazardous materials that are received without proper labeling are impounded in a designated area of the property and will not be released for use until such time as proper labels can be applied. If vendor labels are not available, a special label bearing the information above should be filled out and attached. Portable container labels may be used for this purpose.

D.  Whenever hazardous materials are transferred into portable containers, the person transferring the materials should attach a portable container label to the new container. The label must include the name of the product, identity of the hazardous chemical contained and applicable hazard warnings. If the person transferring the material is uncertain of the identity of the material and the applicable hazard warnings, he/she should contact his/her supervisor.

## MATERIAL SAFETY DATA SHEETS

A.  You will be responsible for maintaining the file of MSDS' at this property. These MSDS' will be kept in the Manager's Office and in the Maintenance Shop and will be organized by product name, which is the same name used in the product label on the container.

B.  You will review the MSDS' as they are received for new information and accuracy. If any parts of the MSDS' are missing or incomplete, You should request a new MSDS from the manufacturer. If the requested new MSDS is not received, You should notify OSHA. If new hazard and/or safety information is received on an MSDS, You is responsible for informing employees of the new information on hazards or safety introduced into their work area.

C.  MSDS' are available to all employees for review during each work shift.

**EMPLOYEE INFORMATION AND TRAINING**

Provide employees with information and training on hazardous chemicals in their work area at the time of their initial assignment.

A. You will be responsible for conducting Hazard Communication training sessions for employees at this property.

B. The Hazard Communication Information and Training Program will be accomplished at this facility through video-taped instruction, discussion of items specific to this property and a written review. You will have a copy of the Hazard Communication Handbook to refer to if employees have any questions.

C. An outline of the training sessions provided at this facility is as follows:

- Explain the OSHA Hazard Communication Standard
- Educate employees about operations in their work area where they may come into contact with hazardous chemicals
- Explain how to read a label for hazard information
- Explain how to recognize a hazard warning
- Review MSDS' and their use
- Explain where and how to access the Written Hazard Communication Program as well as MSDS'

D. Attendance will be recorded for participation in the training session and will be kept on file by the Manager.

E. For information and training about hazards associated with non-routine tasks, see Section VI, titled: Hazards of Non-Routine Tasks.

## LIST OF HAZARDOUS CHEMICALS

A. The list of known hazardous chemicals for this facility will be maintained and located in the MSDS books by You.

B. More information on each hazardous chemical can be found by reviewing the MSDS for that product.

# HAZARDS OF NON-ROUTINE TASKS

A.  It is the policy of this good policy to inform employees of potential hazards associated with non-routine tasks and work and to advise them of the necessary personal protective equipment to accomplish such tasks.

B.  Employees are informed of these hazards by contacting You prior to starting work. Upon contacting You, the following procedure will be followed:

　　1.  Discuss potential hazards of activity

　　2.  Review MSDS of any hazardous chemical involved in the non-routine work 3. Review safety precautions that should be taken during this activity

# ON-SITE CONTRACTORS

A.  It is the responsibility of You to furnish the on-site contractor with the following:

- Description of hazardous chemicals to which contractor's employees may be exposed.

- Suggestions for appropriate protective measures

B.  Likewise, on-site contractors will furnish your Community with the following:

- Description of any hazardous chemicals brought onto the property to which the property employees may be exposed

- Suggestions for appropriate protective measures

C.  The contractor must sign the Contractor Statement that they have read and agree to follow the policy outlines above, that they have been informed of hazardous chemicals to which their employees may be exposed and that they have provided You with the information about any hazardous chemicals being brought onto your Community.

D.  You should reserve the right to stop the work of a contractor if compliance with this policy is inadequate until all applicable safety and health procedures are implemented by the contractor and the contractor is in compliance with your policy.

**ACUTE EFFECT** – An adverse effect on a human or animal, with symptoms developing rapidly and quickly becoming a crisis. See "Chronic Effect."

**ANTIDOTE** – An agent that neutralizes or counteracts the effects of a poison.

**ARTICLE** – A manufactured item:
a. Which is formed to a specific shape or design during manufacture;
b. Which has end use function(s) dependent in whole or in part upon its shape or design during end use; and
c. Which does not release or otherwise result in exposure to a hazardous chemical under normal conditions of use

**ASPHYXIANT** – A chemical gas or vapor that can cause unconsciousness or death by suffocation. Simple asphyxiants, such as nitrogen, either use up or displace oxygen in the air. Chemical asphyxiants, such as carbon monoxide, interfere with the body's ability to receive or use an adequate supply of oxygen.

**BOILING POINT** – The temperature at which liquid changes to a vapor; expressed in degrees Fahrenheit (°F) at sea level pressure. Flammable materials with low boiling points generally present special fire hazards.

**BURNBACK** – The distance a flame will travel from the ignition source back to the aerosol container.

**C.A.S. NUMBER** – Chemical Abstracts Service, a service of the American Chemical Society, identifies particular chemicals with a number.

**CARCINOGEN** – A chemical is considered to be a carcinogen if it is a substance or agent that may cause cancer in animals or humans.

**CHEMICAL** – An element, chemical compound, or mixture of elements and/or compounds.

**CHEMICAL FAMILY** – A group of compounds with related chemical and physical properties, such as ketone or aldehyde family.

**CHEMICAL MANUFACTURER** – An employer with a workplace where chemical(s) are produced for use or distribution.

**CHEMICAL NAME** – The scientific designation of a chemical in accordance with the naming system developed by the International Union of Pure and Applied Chemistry.

**CHRONIC EFFECT** – An adverse effect on an animal or human. Symptoms develop slowly over a long period of time or recur frequently.

**CO$_2$** – Carbon Dioxide. A heavy, colorless, nonflammable and relatively non-toxic gas produced by the combustion and decomposition of organic substances and as a by-product of many chemical processes. Also used as a fire fighting agent.

**COMBUSTIBLE** – A substance capable of fueling a fire. According to OSHA, any liquid having a flash point at or above 100°F and less than 200°F is a combustible liquid.

**COMMON NAME** – Any designation or identification such as code name, code number, trade name, brand name, or generic name used to identify a chemical other than by its chemical name.

**COMPRESSED GAS –**
   a.  A gas or mixture of gases having, in a container, an absolute pressure exceeding 40 psi at 70°F (21.1°C);or
   b.  A gas or mixture of gases having, in a container, an absolute pressure exceeding 104 psi at 130°F (54.4°C) regardless of the pressure at 70°F (21.1°C); or
   c.  A liquid having a vapor pressure exceeding 40 psi at 100°F (37.8°C) as determined by ASTM D323-72.

**CONCENTRATION** – The amount of a substance in a stated unit of mixture or solution. For example, 5 parts (of acetone) per million (parts air). See PPM.

**CONTAINER** – Any bag, barrel, bottle, box, can, cylinder, drum, pipe, reaction vessel, storage tank, or the like that contains a hazardous chemical.

**CORROSIVE** – A substance that, according to the DOT, causes visible destruction or permanent changes in human skin tissue at the site of contact. Or, a liquid that has a severe corrosion rate on steel.

**DECOMPOSITION** – The breakdown of a chemical or substance into different parts or simpler compounds. Decomposition can occur due to heat, chemical reaction, decay, etc.

**DEFATTING** – The removal of natural oils from the skin by fat-dissolving solvent.

**DERMATITIS** – An inflammation of the skin.

**DISTRIBUTOR** – A business, other than a chemical manufacturer or importer, which supplies hazardous chemicals to other distributors or to employers.

**D.O.T.** – The U.S. Department of Transportation (DOT) regulates the transportation of materials.

**EMULSION** – A stable mixture of two or more immiscible liquids held in suspension by small percentages of substances called emulsifiers.

**EVAPORATION RATE** – The rate at which a material is converted to vapor (evaporates) at a given temperature and pressure when compared to the evaporation rate of a given substance. Fast evaporating substances show numbers greater than 3.

**EXPLOSIVE** – A chemical that causes a sudden, almost instantaneous release of pressure, gas and heat when subjected to sudden shock, pressure or high temperature.

**EXPOSURE** – Subjection to a hazardous chemical through any route of entry (inhalation, ingestion, skin contact or absorption, etc.) Also includes potential exposure.

**FLAME EXTENSION** – The distance a flame will travel from the aerosol container when exposed to an ignition source.

**FLAMMABLE** – A material that is easily ignited and burns very rapidly.
   a.  Aerosol, flammable – An aerosol that, when tested, yields a flame projection or a flashback (a flame extending back to the valve) at any degree of valve opening
   b.  Gas, flammable – A gas that, at ambient temperature and pressure, forms a flammable mixture with air at a concentration of 13% volume or less; or a gas that, at ambient temperature and pressure, forms a range of flammable mixtures with air wider than 12% by volume, regardless of the lower limit

c. Liquid, flammable – Any liquid having a flashpoint below 100°F (37.8°C) or higher, the total of which make up 99% or more of the total volume of the mixture

d. Solid, flammable – A solid, other than a blasting agent or explosive that is liable to cause fire through friction, absorption of moisture, spontaneous chemical change, or retained heat from manufacturing or processing, or which can be ignited readily and when ignited burns so vigorously and persistently as to create a serious hazard. A chemical is considered a flammable solid, if when tested, it ignites and burns with a self-sustained flame at a rate greater than 1/10 of an inch per second along its major axis.

**FLAMMABLE LIQUID** – As defined by OSHA, any liquid with a flash point below 100°F.

**FLASH POINT** – The temperature at which a liquid will give off enough flammable vapor to ignite in the presence of an ignition source.

**FORESEEABLE EMERGENCY** – Any potential occurrence such as equipment failure, rupture of containers, or failure to control equipment which could result in an uncontrolled release of a hazardous chemical.

**HAZARD WARNING** – Any words, pictures, symbol or combination on a label which convey the hazard(s) of the chemical(s) in the container(s).

**HAZARDOUS CHEMICAL** – Any chemical that is a physical or health hazard.

**HEALTH HAZARD** – A chemical for which there is statistically significant evidence (based on at least one study conducted in accordance with established scientific principles) that acute or chronic health effects may occur in exposed employees.

**IDENTITY** – Any chemical or common name which is indicated on the Material Safety Data Sheet (MSDS) for the chemical.

**IGNITABLE** – A solid, liquid or compressed gas that has a flash point of less than 140°F; capable of being set on fire.

**IMMEDIATE USE** – The hazardous chemical will be under the control of and used only by the person who transfers it from a labeled container and only within the work shift in which it is transferred.

**IMPORTER** – The first business with employees within the Customs Territory of the United States which receives hazardous chemicals produced in other countries for the purpose of supplying them to distributors or employers within the United States.

**INCOMPATIBLE** – The term used for two substances to indicate that one material cannot be mixed with the other without the possibility of a dangerous reaction.

**INGESTION** – Taking a substance into the body through the mouth.

**INHALATION** – Breathing an airborne substance into the body (lungs), though the nose, mouth and breathing passages. May be in the form of a gas, vapor, fume, mist or dust.

**INHIBITOR** – A substance that is added to another to prevent or slow down an unwanted reaction or change.

**IRRITANT** – A substance that produces an irritating effect when it contacts the skin, eyes, nose or respiratory system.

**LABEL** – Any written, printed or graphic material displayed on or affixed to containers of hazardous chemicals.

**LEL** – Lower Explosive Limit. The lowest concentration of a substance that will produce a fire or flash when an ignition source is present. It is expressed as a percent of vapor or gas in the air by volume. At concentrations below the LEL, the mixture is too "lean" to burn. See UEL.

**MATERIAL SAFETY DATA SHEETS (MSDS)** – Written or printed material concerning a hazardous chemical.

**MELTING POINT** – The temperature at which a solid substance changes to a liquid.

**Mg/m³** – Milligrams per Cubic Meter. Units used to measure air concentrations of dusts, gases, mists and fumes.

**MIXTURE** – Any combination of two or more chemicals if the combination is not, in whole or in part, the result of a chemical reaction.

**mmHG** – Millimeters of mercury. A unit of measure for pressure or partial vacuum that is equal to the height of a column of mercury that this atmosphere will support.

**MUTAGEN** – A substance or agent capable of changing the genetic material of a living cell.

**N/A** – An abbreviation for Not Applicable.

**NARCOSIS** – Stupor or unconsciousness caused by exposure to a chemical.

**NIOSH** – The National Institute for Occupational Safety and Health is a federal agency that trains occupational health and safety professionals, conducts research and tests, certifies respirators, etc.

**ORGANIC PEROXIDE** – An organic compound that contains the bivalent -0-0- structure and which may be considered to be a structural derivative of hydrogen peroxide where one or both of the hydrogen atoms has been replaced by an organic radical.

**OSHA** – The Occupational Safety and Health Administration is a federal agency that publishes and enforces health and safety regulations for most businesses and industries.

**OXIDIZER** – A chemical that initiates or promotes combustion in other materials, thereby causing fire itself or through the release of oxygen or other gases.

**PEL** – Permissible Exposure Limit. An exposure limit established by OSHA as a legal standard. May be a time-weighted average (TWA) limit or a minimum concentration exposure limit.

**pH** – Value that represents the acidity or alkalinity of an aqueous (water-based) solution. Values from 0 to 7 indicate acidity; values from 7 to 14 indicate alkalinity; 7 is neutral

**PHYSICAL HAZARD** – A chemical for which there is scientifically valid evidence that it is a combustible liquid, a compressed gas, explosive, flammable, an organic peroxide, an oxidizer, pyrophoric, unstable or water-reactive.

**PPM** – Parts per million. A unit for measuring the concentration of a gas or vapor in contaminated air. Also used to indicate the concentration of a particular substance in a liquid or solid.

**POLYMERIZATION** – A chemical reaction in which one or more small molecules combine to form larger molecules. A hazardous polymerization is a reaction that takes place at a rate that releases large amounts of energy.

**PYROPHORIC** – A chemical that will ignite spontaneously in air at a temperature of 130°F (54.4°C) or below.

**REACTIVITY** – A substance's tendency to undergo a chemical reaction or change that may result in dangerous side effects, such as explosion, burning, and corrosive or toxic emissions.

**RESPIRATOR** – A device that is designed to protect the wearer from inhaling harmful contaminants.

**SARA** – Superfund Amendments and Reauthorization Act of 1986.

**SENSITIZER** – A substance that may cause no reaction in a person during initial exposure, but to which further exposure will cause an allergic response.

**SOLUBILITY** – The percentage of a material (by weight) that will dissolve in water at a specified temperature.

**SPECIFIC CHEMICAL IDENTITY** – The chemical name, Chemical Abstracts Service (CAS) Registry Number, or any other information that reveals the precise chemical designation of the substance.

**SPECIFIC GRAVITY** – The weight of a material compared to the weight of an equal volume of water; an expression of the density (or heaviness) of the material. Insoluble materials with specific gravity less than 1 will float, an important consideration for fire suppression and spill cleanup.

**TERATOGEN** – A substance or agent to which exposure of a pregnant female can cause malformations in the fetus.

**TLV** – Threshold Limit Value. A term used to express the airborne concentration of a material to which nearly all persons can be exposed day after day without adverse effects.

**TOXIN** – A substance that is poisonous to varying degrees.

**TOXICITY** – The potential of a substance to have a harmful effect and a description of the effect and the conditions or concentration under which the effect takes place.

**UEL** – Upper Explosive Limit. The highest concentration of a substance that will burn or explode when an ignition source is present; expressed in percent of vapor or gas in the air by volume. See LEL.

**UNSTABLE** – A chemical that in the pure state, will vigorously polymerize, decompose, condense or become self-reactive under conditions of shock, pressure or temperature.

**USE** – To package, handle, react or transfer.

**VAPOR** – The gaseous form of substances that are usually liquid or solid.

**VAPOR DENSITY** – The weight of a vapor or gas compared to the weight of an equal volume of air. An expression of density of the vapor or gas. Materials lighter than air have vapor densities less than 1.

Lighter materials tend to rise and dissipate. Heavier vapors are likely to concentrate in low places where they may create fire or health hazards.

**VAPOR PRESSURE** – The pressure exerted by a saturated vapor above its own liquid in a closed container. Vapor pressure is usually expressed as pounds per square inch, but on MSDS is in millimeters of mercury (mmHG) at 68°F. The lower the boiling point of a substance, the higher its vapor pressure.

**VISCOSITY** – A fluid's internal resistance to flow.

**VOLATILE** – The tendency or ability of a liquid to vaporize. Liquids such as alcohol or gasoline are volatile because they have a tendency to evaporate quickly.

**WATER-REACTIVE** – A chemical that reacts with water to release a gas that either is flammable or presents a health hazard.

**WORK AREA** – A room or defined space in a work place where hazardous chemicals are produced or used and where employees are present.